CULTU.

THE REVITALIZATION OF IROQUOIS POTTERY
(Tsi niyokwaliho' da thonu' ya'tit onawatstahla'tu)

TSI'STA LA Rose Skenandore Kerstetter

"Working with Mother Earth gives me a certain closeness that goes beyond a particular art form. It's the grand feeling of knowing the ancestors before have passed through this clay."

— Diane Schenandoah (Oneida, New York)

This book is dedicated to the Iroquois potters of the past, the present, and the future, who are devoted keepers of the traditions.
This Book is also dedicated to all who assisted me as a 102-year-old Potter/Author to complete this book for publication. Special thanks to Adrianna Pelky and Kymberley Pelkey for their technical skills and commitment to the project.
-R.S.K.

FOREWORD:

I first met Rose in the early 1980s when she visited the Cattaraugus Reservation in New York State where I live. She was researching and interviewing Iroquois potters for her upcoming book on pottery.

At that time if you wanted any information about our pottery you had to research the many scholarly, anthropological descriptions written about the subject. There were no Iroquois potters left on our reservations to ask and learn from. The ancient techniques had died with them.

In the subsequent years that Rose continued to research her book, a curious thing was happening. Another, and then another Iroquois potter would emerge. This was a good thing but it would mean that Rose would have to revise and revisit those new potters and add them to her growing book. This new generation of potters is still growing but the book must be written.

Future generations of aspiring Iroquois potters will at least have a reference to start from and someone to ask.

This story is by no means complete and there are still many questions to answer but it is a start of a revival. The continuation of a tradition: a culture in clay.

Peter B. Jones.

INTRODUCTION

As a student at the Institute of American Indian Arts in the late 1970s, I searched for information on traditional Iroquois pottery for guidance and inspiration in preparing to make contemporary pottery and found that there were apparently no books on the subject. I began taking notes from early Bureau of Ethnology Reports (1900s) and bibliographies of books on Iroquois subjects found in the Institute of American Indian Arts (IAIA) Library and the Laboratory of Anthropology at Santa Fe. My original goal in collecting published material on traditional Iroquois pottery was to assemble the selected material in a convenient form of reference for personal use. With a grant from the Southwestern Association for Indian Affairs (the name has since been changed to Southwestern Association for Indian Arts), I was able to purchase printed reports, papers, and books such as *The Archaeology of New York State*. The grant specified a survey was to be made of contemporary Iroquois potters.

Somewhere along the trail it occurred to me that this information might be useful to other potters; and four trips were made to Wisconsin, Canada, and New York State to interview contemporary potters. There was much to learn about Iroquois pottery in its revitalized state. Before I finished the book my perspective had changed to teaching the importance of firmly establishing this tradition in my community at Oneida Wisconsin.

My thanks are extended to the Southwestern Association for Indian Arts for the 1981 grant that began an exciting exploration into the world of Iroquois pottery; to the First People's Fund for two grants that contributed to attaining completion of the book; to the Oneida Tribe of Indians of Wisconsin, The Wisconsin Arts Board, the Oneida Nation Arts Program and the Oneida Nation Veterans Advisory Committee for a grant to produce a CD-ROM. I am grateful to George R. Hamell and Laurence M. Hauptman for their invaluable advice, time and support. Tracy Williams and Denise Sweet and others not mentioned. Yaw^ko to Sara Smith for sharing details of the revitalization beginnings at Six Nations Reserve as well as to all the potters who have helped me to better understand the world of Iroquoian pottery making.

WHERE WE LIVE TODAY

The original homelands of the Six Nations of the Iroquois Confederacy are located in upper New York State, where the Iroquois Nations lived side by side in a symbolic longhouse, with the Seneca as the Keepers of the Western Door; the Mohawk as the Keepers of the Eastern Door; the Onondaga, Keepers of the Central Council Fire; and the Cayuga and the Oneida on either side of the Onondaga as Keepers of the Middle Fires. The Tuscarora joined the Confederacy in the early years of the eighteenth century sponsored by the Oneida. (Hertzberg) 1966:33)

Today the Seneca live on the Allegany, Cattaraugus, and Tonawanda Reservations in New York. The Cayuga reside on the Seneca Reservations and at Six Nations Reserve in Canada. The Oneida live on a reservation near Green Bay, Wisconsin; in Oneida, New York; in London, Ontario, with a few at Six Nations Reserve. The Onondaga live on a reservation near Syracuse and at the Six Nations Reserve. The Mohawk live in Canada at Six Nations Reserve in Ontario; at Kahnawake near Montreal; at Oka in Quebec; and at Tyendinaga Reserve in Ontario; in the United States at Akwesasne on the Canadian-United border, and at Ganienkeh, near Plattsburg, New York. The Tuscarora are located at Lewiston, New York, and a small number live at Six Nations. Additionally, many Iroquois live in and near the larger cities of New York State and in the Ontario and Quebec Provinces of Canada. (Johannsen and Ferguson (1983:viii). A number of Seneca—Cayuga live in a community in northeastern Oklahoma but no Iroquois-style pottery is being produced there. (Bell interview, 1986)

THE REVITALIZATION OF IROQUOIS POTTERY

According to Iroquois oral tradition, small cooking pots were used by the Sky people even before First Woman arrived on Turtle Island.

"On the other side of the sky" relates J. N. B. Hewitt, Tuscarora ethnologist and linguist who has passed on oral tradition through the written word, in the center of the village lived the chief with his wife and daughter. Jealousy of one of the "male man-beings" in the village made the chief ill, and he called for the traditional dream-guessing so that he could recover. Later, as the chief's wife was about to fall through the hole created by uprooting the celestial tree, the "male man-being" handed her "an ear of com, a small mortar and pestle, a small pot, and a bone," which she gathered into her clothing as she began to fall to Turtle Island (Hewitt, 1903:221-254). No description of the pot is given except that it was small. What was its shape, and was it made of bark or clay or some other material? Was it plain or decorated with designs? We can only wonder.

A BRIEF HISTORY OF IROQUOIAN POTTERY ON TURTLE ISLAND

The first inhabitants of the area now known as New York State were migratory hunting groups following the big game animals in the receding Ice Age. When the caribou, the mammoth, and other large animals became scarce, the people supplemented their diet by gathering wild plants and by fishing. Archaeologists have unearthed numerous piles of disintegrated rock, shattered by heat apparently as a result of cooking food in bark, animal skins, or anything that would hold water (Ritchie 1980: 1-3, 60). The women, who were in charge of the cooking, may have been motivated to find a more dependable cooking vessel to replace these containers since they tended to bum up before the food was cooked or fall apart from extensive handling.

For a short period of time—around 1500 BC to l000 BC—carved soapstone (steatite) pots were used for cooking purposes. Made with round or flattened bottoms, the stone pots were round, rectangular, or at times oval in shape, with straight or leaning sides, usually with notched handles at the longer ends. The top edge or rim of the pot was also notched. Sizes ranged from 2" to 6" in height and varied from 6" to 18" in length (Ritchie 1980: 171). They resemble today's casserole dish minus a cover. In spite of its heavy weight, the stone pot must have gained favor for its excellent heat--retaining properties. But for some unknown reason—perhaps weight was involved—the soapstone pottery was rapidly replaced by tempered clay vessels which began to appear throughout New York State and the Northeast around l000 BC (Ritchie 1980: 163).

The earliest true pottery in New York State were rather large, thick vessels with cone-shaped bottoms and straight sides generally exhibiting rounded lips, which were slightly pointed in some pottery. The clay was mixed with large amounts of temper, usually coarse pieces of quartz or ground-up crystalline rock, which may have helped to prevent cracking in the drying stages. Except for cord marking on the inside and outside of the pot, there were no decorative markings. Colors of the fired pottery ranged from buff to gray to black.

Over time, the body of these cone-shaped pots became increasingly rounded, and the out flaring rim changed over to a flattened lip that was occasionally decorated. Later vessels began to show incised line decoration at the rim and neck, followed by shoulder decorations in some instances. The collar width gradually expanded, and both the collar and shoulder displayed incised geometric line designs generally interspersed with rows of circles and/or dots in blank triangular spaces. Each tribe developed its own designs (MacNeish 1952:88).

Clay pottery was used for cooking and storage purposes until replaced with brass and copper kettles by fur traders from Europe in Colonial-era America. By the end of the 17th Century, the Iroquoian tradition of making clay pottery for cooking and storing food had disappeared, along with knowledge of the specialized techniques used in preparing the raw clay. The skill of making Iroquoian pottery lay dormant for about three hundred years before it would be revitalized in a style that would allow the tradition to be carried on. Change is inevitable when a tradition is brought back into use. The ancient forms and designs continue to be used to honor our ancestors. In the revitalization effort, however, emphasis is now placed on the use of iconic and special symbols chosen by the potter to commemorate or honor a special entity, a new tradition which is proving useful to *tsi niyu kwali ho' da* (our ways) in the 21st Century.

IDENTIFYING FEATURES OF A TRADITIONAL IROQUOIS POT

The earliest Iroquoian pottery displayed a simple flaring rim or lip and a constricted neck on a large cone-shaped pot having a capacity of two to twelve gallons (Ritchie, 1980: 291). Early vessels were pinch pots, shaped and smoothed by the paddle and anvil. The pottery evolved into a smaller size with a rounded body, a constricted neck, with wide or high collars through the 15th Century. During this period the coil method dominated pottery production. Low collars are seen on pottery from the 16th and early 17th Centuries (Engelbrecht 2003: 85). Pottery from this era has come to be known as "traditional" pottery. Archaeologists are able to determine which technique was used in making a pot by examining broken pieces of pottery, or sherds. Oneida potters today generally use the coil method to make a pot, but some of the potters also use the pinch pot technique. The process of making a pinch pot as described by Sagard in 1632 is discussed under "Traditional Pottery Making and Firing Techniques".

Early pots mainly had smooth surfaces but were occasionally cord marked, check stamped, or imprinted with a grooved paddle. With the passage of time these surface treatments were used less often, and a smooth surface became the dominant characteristic. The pots were small when the people were migrating groups who gathered their food and the pots became larger when the *Haudenosaunee* (People of the Longhouse) began to cultivate gardens. It became evident that the smaller, thinner-walled pots were best for family cooking purposes as they resisted thermal shock better and cooked food faster. Larger pots were used for quantity cooking. The *Haudenosaunee* occasionally used the uncollared pot form with a thickened lip as storage containers or possibly water drums (Engelbrecht, 2003: 85).

The raised points on the collar, known as castellations, ranged from one to as many as five or more on a pot. Archaeologists refer to a pot with one raised point as a "pitcher pot". No information was found regarding the purpose of castellations on the pottery, but further research may indicate whether they had a utilitarian function or were included purely for design. The traditional pot shows four castellations since most excavated pottery from the 16th or early 17th Century displays four raised points on the collar. Special designs were placed beneath these points.

Three types of castellations as observed in Huron (Iroquoian) pottery are:
  (1) pointed
  (2) bifurcated (divided into two parts or branches)
  (3) squared

The castellation types cited above are used in contemporary pottery.
Appliqued and molded human figures, realistic and abstract faces, "ladder" and other designs are found on much of the ancient Iroquoian pottery. Some early pots display incised gashes around the entire pot immediately under the collar and were decorated at the shoulder in one period of development (MacNeish 1952: 29, 31). Each village with its own pottery designs was constantly exposed to new design ideas through group movements, war captives, and adoption as when a group chose to move their location to another area—which could happen every ten or fifteen years—the designs in the new neighbor's pottery might be adapted and used. Adoption of new members from other tribes, including war captives in some cases, presented opportunities for absorbing new ideas for pottery decoration. (These tendencies provide valuable clues to archaeologists studying tribal group movements.) Natural minerals in the clay body, combined with additions by the potter and the firing process, determined the color of the pot.

TRADITIONAL VS. CLASSIC POTTERY

The term "classic pottery" refers to the prehistoric pottery produced in the early stages of Mohawk cultural development and is classified as "Chance Horizon" pottery since it was first found "by chance" on a farm near Schoharie, New York, in Mohawk country. The pottery sherds from this and allied Mohawk sites uniformly show small-size pottery evolving into larger sizes.

Chance Horizon pottery was carefully crafted and incised, thin walled, and made of well-mixed clay with tempering finer than that ordinarily seen in ancient pottery. Special attention was given to surface smoothing and firing to achieve a well-made pot (Ritchie 1952:6). Holding the actual Chance Horizon sherds in one's hand lends a deep appreciation for the elegance of this finely wrought pottery.

MINIATURE POTS have been found in excavated graves in prehistoric villages in New York State homelands. The tiny pots may have been made by children, and it is possible that some small pots were made to hold herbal and other curative mixtures (Engelbrecht, 2003: 51).

TRADITIONAL IROQUOIS POTTERY MAKING AND FIRING TECHNIQUES

The raw clay used for making early Iroquois cooking pots was first cleaned of organic matter such as sticks, leaves, stones, and other material that could create a defect in the pot wall or explode in the firing. Ethnologist W. H. Holmes in his 1898-99 report, 'Aboriginal Pottery of the Eastern United States', found that the clay in early cooking vessels contained tempering substances that "included pulverized rocks and many mineral substances, powdered shells of mollusks, powdered potsherds, perhaps cinders, ashes of bark, sponge... raw vegetal substances—and sand." But the favorite tempering materials appeared to be "powdered shell and pulverized crystalline rock, mica, iron pyrites, [and] often sand". Holmes further stated "It is not uncommon to see examples in which the paste contains 75 or 80% of the tempering ingredients. Pots were started in "shallow baskets, sections of gourd shell, and vessels of clay or wood shaped for the purpose, to support the pot at the base." Then, to build the pot, "the clay was modeled by 'finger pressure', [the pinch pot technique], or coiling the clay" (Holmes 1898-1899: page   ). George R. Hamell, retired Senior Historian at the New York State Museum, advised that "most... of all prehistoric through 17th Century Iroquois pottery was made by the paddle-and-anvil technique as described by Sagard in 1632. Iroquois potsherds rarely, if ever, show evidence of coil construction" (Hamell, personal correspondence, 1984).

Peter B. Jones, Roger Perkins, Ken Metoxen, and Brenda John are part of a dedicated group of Iroquois potters who are diligently working to reconstruct a clay body with the qualities of a durable cooking pot as found in the ancient clay bodies. Variations in the percentage of temper to clay and other factors are being worked out by these potters. It would be an exciting moment if they discover a formula that would enable a potter to create a pot and fire it outdoors, then cook and serve corn soup from it as it presides over the dining table.

Maybe the potters should try working with Raku, the ancient Japanese technique of adding certain chemicals to earthenware clay to control thermal stress. It seems plausible that further experimentation on raku clay could bring about a clay body that would withstand cooking directly over a fire.

Ha ʔo! Swa te kun'i! — Come! All may eat! This Oneida greeting of hospitality was, no doubt, heard throughout the *Haudenosaunee* homeland for countless generations before the arrival of Columbus. Pots of food were kept cooking over the fire, ready to serve hungry visitors and community members alike. Before clay pots came into use, all of northeastern North America were cooking food in just about any material that would hold water such as bark, animal skins, baskets lined with clay, or wood bowls. The "stoneboiling" method was used to keep the containers from catching on fire.

Gabriel Sagard, a French friar, was sent to Canada in 1632 to convert the Huron Indians, an Iroquoian group, to Christianity.   He became fascinated with the lifeways of these people and recorded many of their customs, including stoneboiling:

"They heated a quantity of stones and gravel red-hot in a good fire, then they threw them into a kettle filled with water in which was the meat or the fish to be cooked, and whenever they took these out they put in others in their place, and in course of time the water was heated and so cooked the meat to some extent" (Wrong, Ed., 1939: 108-109).

Sagard further described details of how Huron pottery was made in 1632, the earliest-known historical reference to the manufacture of Iroquoian pottery:

"But the Hurons and other sedentary tribes and nations used and knew how to make earthenware pots, as they still do, firing them in their ovens. These are very good and do not break when set on the fire even though they may not have water in them ... The women savages make them, taking suitable earth which they sift and pulverize very thoroughly, mixing it with a little sandstone. Then when the lump has been shaped like a ball they put a hole in it with their fist, and this they keep enlarging, scraping it inside with a little wooden paddle as much and as long as is necessary to complete the work. These pots are made without feet and without handles, quite round like a ball, except for the mouth which projects a little" (Wrong, Ed., 1939: 109).

Commenting on Sagard's remarks, the archaeologist Richard S. MacNeish wrote in his work, Iroquois Pottery Types, "Iroquois pottery has grit temper, good paste consistency (when compared with other pottery of the Northeast), the paddle and anvil method of manufacture, an oxidizing process at a low temperature for firing, and a 2 to 4 hardness range" (MacNeish 1952:7).

Much later than Sagard, Eastern Cherokee potter Iwi Katalsta, "the last surviving Iroquoian potter", described the pottery making process to ethnologist M. R. Harrington in 1908. The following description covers the process as given by Iwi Katalsta with an occasional comment included by the author.

Iwi Katalsta used four tools: a hammerstone to pound the clay, a pointed stick for drawing lines and cutting indentations, a smooth river pebble for burnishing, and a carved, broad wooden paddle about 8 inches in length, for stamping her pottery.

Making a ball of clay and holding it in her hands, she put her thumbs together and pressed them into the clay, opening up the walls, thus beginning a pinch pot. She turned the thick-walled base round and round on her wet fingers as she used the wet paddle with the other hand to thin out and shape the bowl contour, which would become the base for her pot, and which she placed in a saucer. Iwi's ancestors may have used a section of gourd or possibly an indentation in wet sand as a base on which to rest the pot. Long, thick coils were used to finish the pot. She placed each coil inside the rim as she built up the pot, but the final coil was placed outside the pot rim and blended in, all this by pinching and blending the coil with her fingers. Then the rim was decorated with Iwi's stick, the body stamped with the paddle, and the pot left to dry. The drying time varied, depending on the weather and the thickness of the pot.

When the pots were dry, Iwi built a hot fire on flat stones buried level with the ground. After warming the pots with the rims nearest the fire, she brushed aside the coals and laid the pots upside down on the hot stones. Stacking bark around the pots and checking to see that the bark was burning, she left it alone for about an hour, after which she removed the pots from the bed of coals with a long stick. Crushed corn cobs were swirled around in the still-hot pot and emptied out, and the coating left on the inside of the pot made it waterproof for cooking purposes. Bran was used if cobs were unavailable (Harrington 1908: 224-226).

In l984 a Pueblo potter in the Southwest, name inadvertently not recorded, shared with the author her technique of "using something sticky like cooked peaches" to coat the insides of her pots "to close the pores" and make them waterproof.

Since the Cherokee people are Woodland Indians and have linguistic connections with the Seneca Iroquois, it would seem advantageous for modern Iroquoian potters to study closely the Cherokee methods of making pottery and firing.

Harrington's l908 report signaled the apparent end of traditional Iroquoian pottery making. However, in 1985 the author took an 8-day pottery workshop with Dr. John K. White, a member of the Chickamauga Band of Cherokee, an anthropologist and traditional Cherokee potter, at his studio in Michael, Illinois. Dr. White stated there were no breaks by Cherokee potters in their traditional pottery making and firing techniques.   He had learned to make pottery at age eleven from his Great Aunt Sally Hicks, a Cherokee traditional potter and Indian doctor of the Ani-gi-lo-hi Clan of the Chickamauga Band of Cherokee from Eastern Tennessee. Believed to be in her early nineties when she died in 1951 or 1952, Sally was a contemporary of Eastern Cherokee Iwi Katalsta, whose pottery making techniques were described by Harrington. Sally made the identical complicated, stamped, flat-bottom vessels that could be used to boil medicines on top of a cook stove as recorded by Harrington for Iwi Katalsta.

At the workshop, White and eight potters including the author, gathered clay from White's land in Michael, Illinois; and after cleaning and testing the clay, the potters made their own tools. The next day White and the workshop participants each handbuilt a Cherokee pot (the author made an Iroquois pot), using the coil method and handmade tools and paddles to smooth, cord mark, and decorate the pot. At the end of the week, the pottery was fired and left in the pit overnight so that they would be cool enough to be safely handled by the workshop participants when they picked up their fired pots the next day.

White's pots were used at times for family cooking purposes and were considered very satisfactory for this purpose, some having been in use for up to five years. White does not sell his pottery, preferring to use them as gifts. Interest and involvement in the revival of native cultures led White to study the archaeological records and ethnographic accounts, leading to teaching traditional ceramic workshops for groups of Native Americans involved in the preservation of their culture, as well as specific tribal groups, including the Six Nations Iroquois at Brantford, Ontario (White, 1985, personal communication).

"The pots are alive and have a soul, and what makes me feel good is that I feel these ancient potters are helping to guide my hands" (White, 1985, personal communication).

O na wat sta la' tu (clay) was gathered from local deposits. The colors of fired clay range from buff through gray to tan, reddish brown, and dark brown, due to the minerals, sand, and other components found in particular areas. Dried-out clay had to be pounded with something heavy like a large stone to break it down fine enough to be able to clean out the twigs, leaves, stones, and other organic matter.   Next, temper was added if needed. Finally, water was added to achieve the right consistency to work the clay. The test was in the firing, when cracks might appear in the clay, indicating that more sand, pulverized quartz, or ground shell needed to be added to the wet clay. Over time, experimentation and adjustments to the composition of the clay became intuition. Potters developed a feel for the balance that yielded a workable clay body.

Peter B. Jones, an Onondaga potter from the Onondaga Reservation in New York, has been studying Iroquois pottery for over forty years. In 2006 Pete came to Oneida to teach his technique for handling clay freshly dug from the ground and to demonstrate his method of firing outdoors. A large pot had to be handled separately from the firing of much smaller pottery brought by the participants, and Pete "flash fired" it, a much faster technique but with exquisite results.

(Mention should be made of Pete's hilarious "cloud-diverting axe ceremony", only relied on in direly-desperate circumstances such as the sudden appearance of fast-approaching darkly-menacing rain clouds. In this case, the ceremony turned the major rainstorm away, allowing only a few drops of rain to fall and granting a successful firing!) The workshop was energizing and exciting for the participants, apparent by their remarks made at the closing.

THE TRADITIONAL VS. THE CONTEMPORARY POTTER

In ancient times, the men took care of the hunting, while the women were in charge of the households, the gardens and the cooking. This strongly indicates that women made the pottery. Today, hunting and pottery making have become options for the use of our leisure time: A woman may now enjoy hunting as a hobby, and a man may choose to cook for the family, work professionally as a chef, and even create a career as a potter.

In the past, the Iroquois woman learned to make pottery by observing her mother. Perhaps, as a child, she shaped small pots and watched them being fired. Thus, she learned to make pottery in the traditional style of her clan or village. Natural materials from her local environment were used: clay, a few stones, ground shell, quartzite, sand, perhaps a gourd for a pot base, a stick cut from a branch and wrapped with inner tree fibers that had been rolled into rope for cord marking, a sharp bone or wood implement for incising, and some water.

Today's potter on the other hand, simply opens the plastic bag, cuts off some clay, kneads it a bit to remove any air bubbles, and it is ready for use! The benefits of modem technology are far-reaching. The availability and convenience of prepared materials including clays, glazes, temperature cones, ready-made tools, the electric wheel, electric and gas kilns, the pug mill and more, are time and labor saving devices. The technology of weather forecasting helps in choosing the best day for firing outdoors.

Iroquoian potters today include women and men who use both techniques of hand building and the potter's wheel, but a larger number prefer hand building, which seems to soften and mellow the contours of the pottery. For many potters, the wheel is also useful for building up an inventory of "bread and butter" items—smaller, quickly produced, and lower-priced pieces to help pay the bills while working on works of art that take more time to finish.

The *Haudenosaunee* potters create contemporary pottery in a decorative style as well as replicating traditional pottery. The use of both styles keeps our rich cultural heritage foremost in our daily lives and reminds us of who we are and where we come from.

EXPLORING THE MEANING OF SOME POTTERY DESIGNS

All six tribes of the Iroquois Confederacy—Seneca, Cayuga, Onondaga, Oneida, Mohawk, and Tuscarora—basically use the same techniques and methods for making their pottery; the differentiation is found mainly in the decoration on the collar. Various influences such as group movements, war captives, and adoption were factors in bringing changes to pottery designs. Careful study of these changes on prehistoric and historic pottery collars has aided the archaeologist in achieving a clearer picture of contacts with other tribes in defining the routes of village migrations. While some symbols and designs on pottery are identifiable today, the meaning of a selected symbol by the ancient Iroquoian potter has become lost knowledge in a great many instances.

The author discovered an interesting full-figure human effigy design under the castellation of a pot in a Bureau of Ethnology Report and used it often on pottery. It became a favorite, but what was most exciting was when research revealed it was an Oneida design.

The book, "Iroquois Pottery Types", describes that design as "2 to 7 horizontal lines at the center of the decorating space on the collar and continuing around the pot, with vertical or oblique lines incised down to meet the horizontal lines. Below the horizontal lines is another row of vertical or oblique lines incised around the entire collar." Archaeologists have classified this type as Thurston Horizontal.

"Often on pots of this type from historic sites there are human effigies under the castellations. The head is round with the facial features fairly distinct; the body is short and rectangular, usually with closely-spaced horizontal lines crossing it. The arms extend out and downward from the body and are indistinct; they also are crossed by horizontal incisions. In rare cases, one arm is flexed and the forearm raised with the palm of the hand facing the front, or the hands are on the hips. The legs extend straight down from the body. Often the lower legs extend below the collar, while the thigh is on the collar. This gives the legs a slightly flexed appearance. The feet may come together or be slightly apart. The legs are also crossed by horizontal incisions. The entire figure (except the head) is composed of limbs and a body which are definitely rectangular and conventionalized. No attempt seems to have been made to reproduce actual body contours or dimensions. Oblique incisions sometimes appear on the shoulders of pots of this type." Most pots in this category displayed two castellations, with collars averaging one and one-half inches wide, ranging from one inch to two and one-half inches. (MacNeish, 1952: 66, 68)

An interesting interpretation for a possible meaning behind the faces and the full-figure effigies found under some castellations on Iroquoian pots has recently been presented by Anthony Wonderley, Oneida Nation Historian, New York. Wonderley's interpretation of the above-mentioned effigies suggests a ritual relationship between Oneida women as food providers and "a mythological race of corn husk people", who work together to complete the corn harvest. Wonderley further proposes "that effigies make sense as evidence of a covenant between human women and non-human beings, presumably corn husk people and explains that making pottery depicting this aspect may be the Oneida way of offering gratitude and thankfulness to these helpers who continue to assist us in successfully harvesting our o n^ ste (corn). Note that human effigy faces and figures on pottery are found in other regions of Iroquoia as well (Wonderley, 2002:24,25,26).

Wonderly's proposal suggests to the author the concept of perhaps making special longhouse ceremonial use of the Oneida pot with human effigies, thereby acknowledging thankfulness to these faithful helpers for their assistance in harvesting the com and other crops as the Three Sisters, com, beans, and squash, continue to sustain the Oneida people throughout the year.

In 1934 conditions seemed favorable for a revitalization of Iroquois pottery when Arthur C. Parker, a New York State archaeologist and of Seneca descent, began a revival of traditional arts and crafts on the Seneca Reservation. Parker's plan, known as the WPA Arts Project, was to revive the declining interest in the arts and crafts and at the same time create employment opportunities for Tonawanda and Cattaraugus community members in the Great

Depression era. Pottery was not included because no one on the staff at Rochester Museum could be found who could make a traditional pot!

The 1960s and 1970s was a period of national upheaval and civil unrest resulting from world and national events that included the Vietnam War and its protests, the civil rights movement, the hippie rebellion, the assassinations of John F. Kennedy, Robert Kennedy, and Dr. Martin Luther King, Jr., the Alcatraz takeover, along with other significant issues and events. There arose during this time a strong cultural rebirth and interest in the traditional native arts in the United States. Pottery is one of the listed crafts in Native American Art in the Twentieth Century: Makers, Meanings, Histories that were affected by the substantial change in how Native art was being viewed. Two Santa Fe traders during this period stimulated the growing momentum of gallery owners and museum curators who were beginning to educate museum visitors and art patrons to view Native American art as works of fine art in addition to their ethnographical interest {Rushing (editor): 1999, Chapter 4 Bernstein: 57-68). In this tumultuous era, the Institute of American Indian Arts (IAIA) was established in 1962 in Santa Fe, New Mexico, a two-year art college granting the Associate of Fine Arts degree.

IAIA is today a four-year college located on a 140-acre campus, with a student body representing over 75 tribes. Iroquoian pottery has experienced a long journey from its utilitarian usage by our ancestors to the place it holds today in the fine arts field.

THE REVITALIZATION OF IROQUOIS POTTERY

(Photo Elda Smith at the Pottery Wheel)

ELDA SMITH, (Mohawk) (1919-1976) is credited with the revitalization of traditional Iroquois pottery. Her attentive study of pottery collections in the Ontario Museum and other museums, as indicated in the dark finish resembling smoke firing and the use of traditional design elements in seeking to retain the essence of the ancient pieces, has influenced three generations of family and community members to continue the work she initiated.

In 1961 ELDA "Bun" SMITH, (Mohawk) (1919-1976), with the devoted   support of her husband, OLIVER SMITH (Mohawk) (1911-1979), gathered family members and friends at their home on Sour

Springs Road in Hagersville on the Six Nations Grand River Reserve in Ontario, Canada, to begin a series of pottery workshops that included use of the pottery wheel and hand building. Tess Kidick, a professional potter, was the instructor for these workshops. The Smith home became the center of activity for pottery making. A year later, Elda and Oliver Smith opened a studio there for the production of Mohawk pottery.

For the next l5 years, ELDA SMITH successfully operated Mohawk Pottery, working full time at the wheel while supervising 15 potters. Her studio was equipped with 12 wheels, ten of which were electric, in addition to one treadle and one kick wheel. Mohawk Pottery was fired at 2300 degrees F. Natural clay found on the Smiths' land was used until it was determined that using commercial clay was the better choice for their production needs. Elda worked out a special formula for the clay wash used on the exterior of the pottery (Sara Smith, 1985, personal communication). Elda Smith became widely known for a wheel-thrown pot that was covered over by a second thrown pot designed with decorative cut-out openings exposing the inner pot.

(Edla Smith double wall Pot ca 1967)

Awards and honors for her work include a Centennial Medal, and her pottery is in the Smithsonian Collection as well as the Collection of the Royal College in London. In 1967 she was invited to present her pottery to Queen Elizabeth II, who attended Expo' 67 in Montreal. Elda's pottery was also exhibited in Expo '70 in Japan. (Sara Smith, 1985, personal communication).

(Photo Elda Smith w/pot presented to Queen Elizabeth II in 1967)

The pot Elda holds in the photograph has a softly angled collar with a check stamped body displaying the Hiawatha and other wampum belts as well as various Iroquois cultural images, all contributing to an elegant gift for the Queen. This event is a memorable highlight of Elda Smith's distinguished career.

OLIVER SMITH (1911-1979) used the wheel to create variations on the traditional pottery styles. He had a distinct flair for designing and creating small pottery items such as pipes and figurines. Much of his time and support were involved with the sale and promotion of Mohawk Pottery, in addition to his responsibilities as principal of a local school (Sara Smith, 1985, personal communication).

Oliver Smith (Mohawk)
Vase, wheel thrown, n.d.

(Photo Oliver Smith pot)

(Photo Oliver Smith at the pottery wheel)

Mohawk Pottery continued production until Elda Smith's death in 1976, after which the Smith family potters set up their own studios on Sour Springs Road in Hagersville, Ontario, probably around 1976-77.

SARA SMITH, daughter of Elda and Oliver Smith, became interested in working with clay in the 1960s, working mostly in "freeform".   With her mother's encouragement, she studied with Rinaldo Sciannella, the renowned Italian potter residing in Ontario at the time.   Since l975, Sara has produced wheel thrown pottery in her studio, Turtle 'n Dove, on the Six Nations Reserve (Sara Smith, l985, personal communication). Her work is widely known in the United States, Canada, and Europe.

Sara employs glazes on the inside of her stoneware pottery, which exhibits a dark stain on the outer surface. A high-fire kiln is used. Sara's pottery is characterized by controlled, highly detailed, strong incising. Most of her pot forms show a rounded body building up from the flat base to a slightly curving neck, then flaring into a modified collar. The pottery suggests shapes of some prehistoric pots found in Ontario, but her pots are mainly contemporary, usually combining personal designs with traditional. Strong design is, undoubtedly, Sara's forte.

In recent years she has turned to a more relaxed way of life as manager of a gift shop in nearby Ohsweken on the Reserve, but she may have left the door open a crack with her remark, "Once a potter, always a potter." Whatever the future holds, Sara will leave a lasting mark on the pottery world as a superbly talented Mohawk potter.

Sara Smith has exhibited her pottery at Canada House Gallery in London, the McKenzie Gallery and the Royal Ontario Museum in Canada. Her pottery is in the collections of the McMichael Collection, the Ojibway Cultural Foundation, The Whetung Ojibway Crafts, the Woodland Indian Cultural Educational Centre in Canada, and the Native American Center for the Living Arts in the United States (Sara Smith, 1985, personal communication).

(Photo Sara pot)

(Photo Sara Smith at the Pottery Wheel)

STEVEN T. SMITH (Mohawk) the son of Elda and Oliver Smith, and his wife, potter LEIGH SMITH, (Mohawk), originated Talking Earth Pottery. (Sara Smith, 1985, personal communication). Steve has emerged as one of the foremost working potters in Canada. Leigh Smith has a pottery piece in the collection of Margaret Thatcher, former Prime Minister of England.

(Photo Steve's turtle pot)

(Photo Leigh's Thatcher pot)

SANTEE SMITH, daughter of Steve and Leigh Smith, is a pottery designer at Talking Earth Pottery when she is not engaged in her professional career as choreographer-artistic director of *Kaha':wi* (She Carries) Dance Theatre.

(Photo Santee pot)

SEMIAH SMITH, daughter of Santee Smith and great granddaughter of Elda Smith, is learning firsthand the steps in creating Iroquois pottery as she personally checks out the studio routines of her potter grandparents at Talking Earth Pottery. She is shown in a 1996 photograph at the age of two-and-a-half with a pot she had decorated. She will be a fourth generation potter in the family if she follows the path originated by her great grandmother.

(Photo Semiah Smith at age 2-1/2 with pot)

SYLVIA SMITH, sister of Elda, set up her own studio, Kanyengeh (People of the Flint) Pottery around 1977. Some of the people who had been working in Elda's workshop moved to Sylvia's studio to work: Joanne Smith, Dee Martin (d), Anne Scott, and Thelma Beaver (d), among others. I purchased a signed Sylvia Smith pot with a turquoise glazed interior in the late 1960s at a shop on the Reserve. It was difficult to choose from the variety of pottery forms and sizes displayed; each piece bore the dark stain on the outside, while the interior joyfully announced its presence with a bright glaze. There was a huge array of colors-I remember seeing brilliant blues, reds, yellows, purples, greens as well as gray. They worked well as a contrast to the quiet exteriors and could easily be designated as "jewel pots".

Sylvia Smith is presently living in Brantford, Ontario, and continues to make pottery with her daughter-in-law, Joanne Smith, at Joanne's studio in Oshawa, Ontario (Sylvia Smith, 1996, personal communication).

(Photo Sylvia pot)

DARLENE L. SMITH (1936-2001), a non-Native potter married to a Mohawk, was part of the original Smith family living on the Grand River Reserve in Canada in the late 1960s and early 1970s. Darlene learned to make pottery from Elda Smith and became well known for her elegant wheel-thrown miniature pottery incised at the collar, stained and fired at cone 3, which she also used for larger pots. After living in California for a time, she later moved back to Six Nations, where she resided until her death in 2001. Three daughters and a granddaughter are carrying on the tradition at Earth 'N Fire Pottery, the studio of Darlene's youngest daughter, Kari Smith, at Sheguiandah, Ontario (Wanda Smith, 2001, personal communication).

When I visited the family of Darlene Smith following her death, her two older daughters, Wanda Smith and Cindy Henhawk, with granddaughter, Jessica Henhawk, also a potter, presented me with a gift of two miniature pots made by Darlene and a 4-1/2" high memorial pot honoring their mother. The card accompanying the pot reads as follows: "This piece of pottery is one of a limited edition created by Darlene L. Smith. Darlene was known for her intricate Iroquoian decorating technique which adorned all pottery she created. This piece of pottery is unique in that it is one of the last hand thrown pieces of her career (1965-2001), yet unadorned with design due to an invading illness. These pieces were then completed by her daughters. (2001). *** Darlene celebrated the completion of her earthly life on June 30, 2001 ***" (Wanda Smith, 2001, personal communication). It was a lovely gesture of acknowledging the esteem enjoyed by their mother and grandmother.

(Photo Darlene pot w/miniature pots)

MURRAY ANTONE, (19 -19) (Oneida of the Thames) lived in Southwold, Ontario. In 1989-90, Murray Antone, LuAnn Smith-John and Simon Elijah, Jr., Oneidas from Southwold, went to Six Nations Grand River Reserve for sixteen weeks to learn traditional pottery making from Darlene Smith (April Antone, l996, interview). Murray's work is influenced by the early Mohawk Pottery—his wheel-thrown pots are dipped in a dark brown stain before firing, the pot interiors are usually glazed in bright, opaque colors, and the decorations on the pottery carry some of the individualized geometric designs seen in the early work of the Smith potters.   Pastel colors over white clay was used in designing some of his pieces, examples of which can be seen in the collection of the Oneida Nation Museum (April Antone, 1996, personal communication).

(Photo Murray pot)

APRIL ANTONE, (Oneida of the Thames), lives in Southwold and is a niece of Murray Antone, with whom she apprenticed. Her wheel thrown pottery is also similar to the Smiths' early work. She creates wheel thrown traditional-style miniature pots complete with "jewel-tone" color glazes on the interior of the pots. April has requested an apprenticeship with the author to learn hand building, which she feels "will help to make my pottery more authentic".

(Photo April pot with miniature pots)

PETER B. "Pete" JONES, (Onondaga), is a world-class potter and sculptor from the Onondaga Reservation in New York State. No stranger to clay, he has worked with it ever since he was four or five years of age, creating figurines from clay brought to him by family members and friends. His studies of prehistoric and historic pottery in New York State museums led to a lifelong interest in Iroquois pottery. After graduating in 1965 from high school at IAIA in Santa Fe, New Mexico, Peter was a student teacher in the ceramics department in hand building techniques including ceramic sculpture and wheel thrown pottery under the mentorship of Ottalie Loloma, famed Hopi potter. He graduated in 1968 from IAIA, which had become a 2-year art college in 1962. Pete began to research Iroquois pottery in 1977 after returning to Onondaga. Using the coiling technique and the pottery wheel, he creates traditional and contemporary styles of Iroquois pottery as well as sculptures in clay and bronze. He has numerous pottery workshops, demonstrations, and exhibitions to his credit. One of the highlights of his outstanding career was a commission to create two heroic-size sculptures of Native Americans, each carrying a canoe on his back, for the northern and southern ends of the historic Akron, Ohio, Portage Path. In 2012 a special exhibit of Peter B. Jones' work titled was part of IAIA's 50th anniversary Exhibit (Peter B. Jones, 2013, personal communication).

(Photo Akron Ohio sculptures)

(Photo Peter B. Jones pot)

44

His hand built traditional pots remain faithful to the ancient forms and incised designs while carrying the stamp of his personal style and are further enhanced by the final smoke firing outdoors.

Pete came to Oneida in 2006 to lead a 5-day workshop that included locating clay deposits at Oneida, preparing the clay for use, and demonstrating traditional firing. The Oneida Nation Arts Program had provided a map showing locations of clay deposits on the reservation, and Pete processed natural clay in preparation for making pottery. Chasing down those clay deposits was an exciting adventure especially when we discovered the exemplary qualities of the clay found at Stagger Lane and the hilarity it created at this site with its own special history. In fact, Stagger Lane clay turned out to be one of the best clays discovered that day. On the final day of the workshop, Pete's firing demonstration was an amazing, informative, and downright fun experience!

ROSE KERSTETTER (Oneida) is an enrolled member of the Oneida Nation of Wisconsin. Around 1965 while living in Granby, Connecticut, Rose began to experiment with making Iroquois pottery following a series of visits viewing traditional pottery in museums of New York State. Never satisfied with the results, she nevertheless plodded on with a dream of one day holding a pot in her hands, as her ancestors did, to check out its heft, thickness, size, and decoration, free of the ever-present museum glass panel between her and the pot. She turned a small basement room in her home into her first workspace, Running Deer Studio, and worked on pottery there on weekends. In 1970, she moved to Embudo, New Mexico, where she subsequently studied ceramics at IAIA, graduating at the age of sixty in 1979 with an Associate of Fine Arts Degree in Ceramics and Three-dimensional Design.

With a 1983 grant from the South Western Association for Indian Affairs (now called South Western Association for Indian Arts), she made four visits to museums and potters in New York State and Canada to research information that might be helpful in retaining the integrity of the ancient pottery in her contemporary work. The 1996 move back to her home community of Oneida, Wisconsin, provided an excellent opportunity to teach pottery workshops that introduced the revitalized tradition. It was an attempt to make pottery as popular as the embedded crafts of jewelry, beadwork, com husk dolls, and baskets, among other traditional Oneida arts.

Highlights of her career include a blue ribbon for a traditional Iroquois pot at Indian Market, Santa Fe, New Mexico, (1979); a contemporary pot on permanent display at the New York State Museum (1988); Wisconsin Indian Traditional Art Invitational, University of Wisconsin/Stevens Point, 1990, 1989, First Place 1987, 1986.

(Photo Rose Pot)

MICHAEL JONES (Onondaga descent) is the son of Peter B. Jones. On a family visit in 1982, Michael, age nine at the time, displayed a surprising array of pots he had made. Over the years since then, his talent has been carefully nurtured by his father, and after attending IAIA, Michael is today a second generation potter, successfully blending the traditional with his own personal visions. Michael, who is also a musician, lives with his wife and two children in New Braunfels, Texas.

(Photo Michael pot)

While living in New Mexico, the author learned of two Oneida (Wisconsin) college students who were researching Iroquois pottery: Kenneth B. Metoxen and Brenda John. They were immediately contacted to compare notes on how they were handling the contemporary perspective.

In the summer of l984, KENNETH B. METOXEN (Oneida) apprenticed to Rose Kerstetter before enrolling at IAIA to study ceramics. He graduated with honors from IAIA, earning an Associate of Fine Arts Degree in 3-dimensional design and museum studies in 1986, then went on to the University of Wisconsin/Oshkosh, graduating with a Bachelor of Science Degree in Arts, followed by a Master of Arts and a Master of Fine Arts Degree in Sculpture from UW/Madison. He has attained international attention as the Oneida sculptor who established the annual Sculpture Symposium at Oneida in 2002. This is an invitational event, and sculptors arrive each summer from Europe, Japan, other foreign countries, and the United States (Kenneth B. Metoxen, 2010, personal communication). Metoxen's pottery exhibits his passion for the sculptural form. With a grant from First People's Fund in 2012, Metoxen opened Peace Stone Studio, where a variety of clay items may be purchased, including large Iroquois pots. Metoxen's favorite sport, lacrosse, is depicted on many of his clay creations, including pottery.

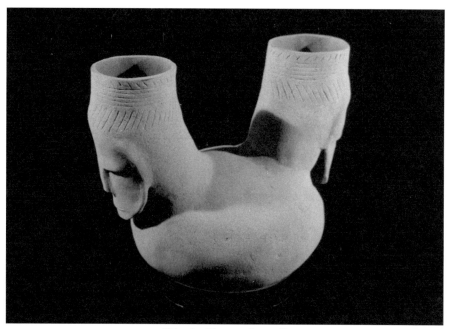

(Photo Kenneth pot)

BRENDA JOHN (Oneida) began to research Iroquois pottery beginning in 1993 as a college student. Following graduation from college, Brenda decided to concentrate on Iroquois pottery. Using white stoneware clay, her contemporary pottery is marked by delicately incised work on the pot collar and rounded bottom of the traditional form. She sold her pottery at the juried Eiteljorg Art Market at Indianapolis in 2005. Brenda works full time for the Oneida Tribe and continues to make outstanding pottery, which was available at Bear Paw Art Gallery, also known as Bear Paw Keepsakes, in Green Bay until the Gallery closed its doors on October 3l, 2012.

(Photo Brenda Pot)

JENNIFER M. STEVENS (Oneida) had attended one of the author's workshops previous to receiving an apprenticeship in the fall of 2002 for further study with Kerstetter through a Traditional Native Arts Apprenticeship grant from the Wisconsin Arts Board. Stevens returned to college to study for the Bachelor of Arts Degree in Fine Arts with a focus on ceramics at St. Norbert College in DePere, Wisconsin. As an emerging artist, Jennifer's rich, contemporary style is a valuable asset in her fast-evolving rise in the art world. Her latest ceramics and paintings were shown at Bear Paw Gallery, also known as Bear Paw Keepsakes, until the Gallery closed its doors on October 3l, 2012.

Stevens is also a trained lyric soprano vocalist, active in recitals and other events in the community and nationwide.

(Photo Jennifer pot)

HOW STABLE IS THE ART FORM?

Revitalized by Mohawk potter Elda Smith in 1961, traditional pottery is slowly returning to its place as one of the practicing traditions at Oneida after an absence of about 300 years of non-use.

No clay cooking pots were tucked in the baggage of the Oneidas when they moved from New York State to Wisconsin during the period of 1823-1826. It was assumed that the oral tradition of passing down from generation to generation the formulas for making the clay durable, the techniques for making and firing them, as well as any related pottery stories had disappeared forever. At the 2007 Oneida History Conference Dr. Clifford Abbott, professor of linguistics at the University of Wisconsin/Green Bay, who has studied the Oneida language for thirty years, was asked if there were any references made to our ancestors' cooking in clay pots in the stories that were written by a group of Oneida writers in the 1940-42 Oneida Language and Folklore Project directed by Dr. Floyd Lounsbury. These stories were written either in English or in the Oneida language about life in the Oneida community during the years of the Great Depression (Hauptman and McLester 1999: 64). Abbott stated that no mention was made of clay cooking pots in the stories although there were references to basket making and beadwork. (Abbott, 2007, personal communication).

Attempting to re-introduce and expand a lost tradition will take time, patience, and persistent nurturing. It will, however, return in a modified style. Since the pots are no longer used as cooking ware, contemporary artists choose to create new decorative versions that display elements of the ancient pottery shapes and incising as a way of expressing honor and gratitude to those venerable potters who made and used the original pots to sustain their families. The traditional forms of the ancient pottery will continue to be replicated to keep them vividly alive.

The evening workshops previously mentioned were useful as a first step in the revitalization effort. They were well received and served as, first, an introduction to a part of Oneida history that many community members were not aware of, and secondly, instruction on how to create the forms and incised designs of the ancient pottery. Throughout those workshop years, a delightful sense of excitement and high interest in the participants of the workshops prevailed. There were two workshops per year for 3 consecutive years, with 10 participants in each class. That undertaking produced an Oneida potter, Jennifer M. Stevens, who makes pottery on a regular basis and is now teaching the craft. Following her apprenticeship with the author beginning in 2002, Jennifer taught traditional pottery workshops for adults in Oneida and at area elementary schools and continues working full-time for the Tribe. Her dedicated efforts will undoubtedly inspire other artists in promoting the art form to the level of popularity seen in basket making, bead working, jewelry making and other traditional arts at Oneida. Stevens' pottery workshops are sponsored by the Oneida Nation Arts Program.

The youth in our community may well be the catalyst in the revitalization of this ancient tradition in Wisconsin. Traditional pottery classes are being made accessible to the youth of our community at the Tribal Schools, and classes are available occasionally at the Family Recreation Center in Oneida. The Oneida Nation Museum displays and sells contemporary pottery, and two Oneida artists are selling pottery from their studios.

Immediate connections are made with Mother Earth and our ancestors when we make a pot from clay and reflect that it was used long ago for cooking food—maybe corn soup or perhaps storing dried beans. We can retain those positive connections in our hearts and minds by diligently keeping the tradition alive for "those faces yet to come out of the ground", knowing the next Seven Generations will find the living culture that supports us in our daily living will be available to them in a strong and viable form.

It is sincerely hoped that this introduction to traditional Iroquois pottery and its revitalization will encourage more potters, young and old, from the six tribes of the Iroquois Confederacy, to make pottery for their homes and as gifts, a tradition that will continue to be a strong link to remaining *Haudenosaunee* forever.

CULTURE IN CLAY: THE REVITALIZATION OF IROQUOIS POTTERY

GLOSSARY:

April Antone
Douglas Beaver
Carol Cornelius
Sis Falcone
Brenda Hill
Scott Hill
Brenda John
Michael Jones
Peter B. Jones
Rose Kerstetter
Amanda Malcolm
Kenneth B.Metoxen
Don Monture
Ron Monture
Carol Moses
Roger Perkins
Molly Melchert Powless
Dan Skenandore
Diane Shenandoah (Oneida, NY)
Sara Smith
Steven T. Smith
Leigh Smith
Santee Smith
Semiah Smith (child)
Sylvia Smith
Jennifer Stevens
Tammy Tarbell-Boeh
Elda Smith (deceased)
Oliver Smith (deceased)
Darlene Smith (deceased)
Murray Antone (deceased)

1. **April Antone**

April Antone 7 Various Pots

April Antone Carving Turtle Pot

April Antone Jar with Long Neck

April Antone Turtle Pot

2. Douglas Beaver

Douglas Beaver Round Pot with Collar

3. Carol Cornelius

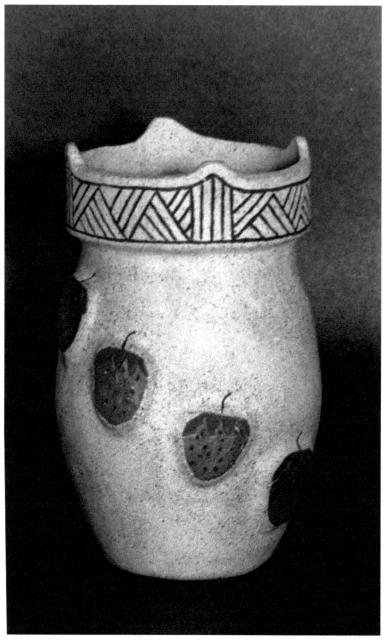

Carol Cornelius Collared Pot with Strawberries

Carol Cornelius Collared Pot with Thunderclouds

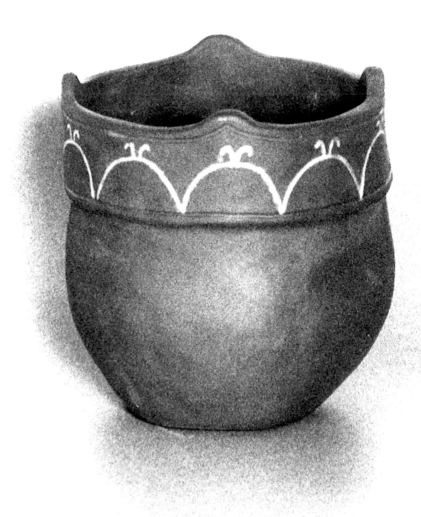

Carol Cornelius Small Pot with Skydome on Collar

Carol Cornelius with Pot

4. **Sis Falcone**

Sis Falcone At-Home Kiln

Sis Falcone Figure of Skywoman with Twins

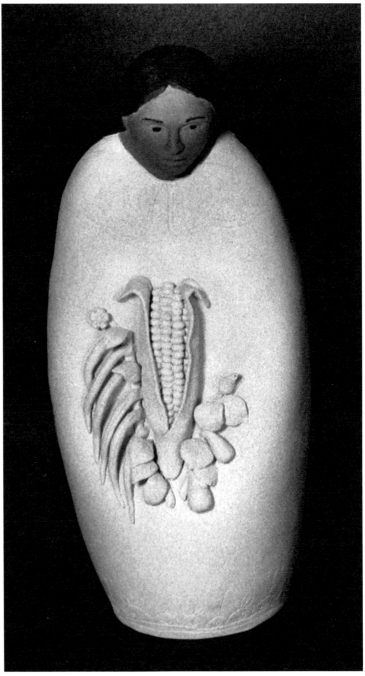

Sis Falcone Figure with Corn, Beans, and Squash

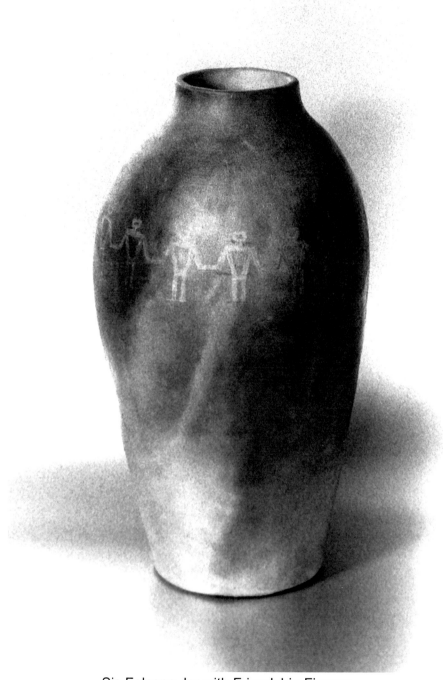

Sis Falcone Jar with Friendship Figures

Sis Falcone Pot with Bear Comb Design at Top

Sis Falcone Pot with Fire Clouds

Sis Falcone Squash Pot with Three Sisters at Top

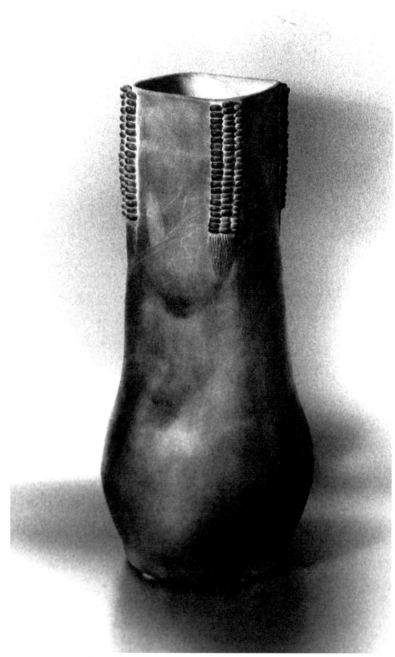

Sis Falcone Tall Jar with Corn Pattern

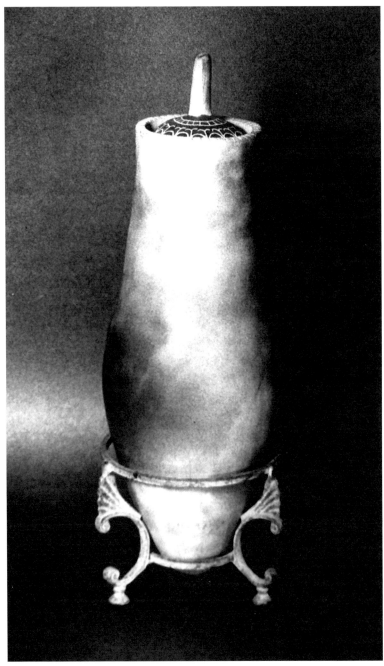

Sis Falcone Tall Jar with Lid

Sis Falcone White Pot with Sky Dome around Collar

5. Brenda Hill

Brenda Hill Forming Pot

Brenda Hill Pot with Collar

Brenda Hill Pot with Rounded Collar

Brenda Hill Pot with Short Collar

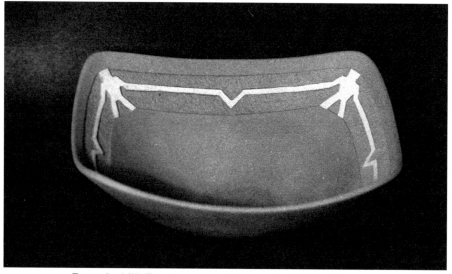

Brenda Hill Rectangular Bowl with White Figures

Brenda Hill Turtle Figure

6. Scott Hill

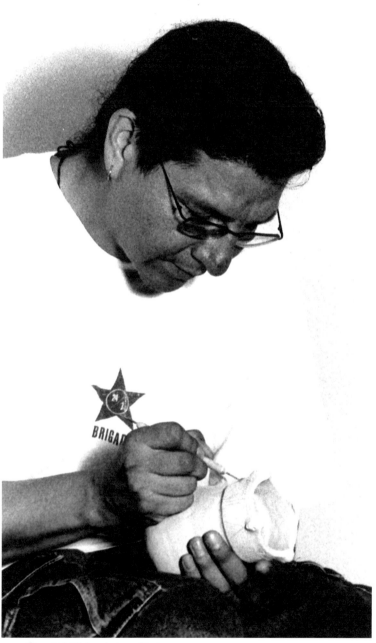

Scott Hill Incising Pot

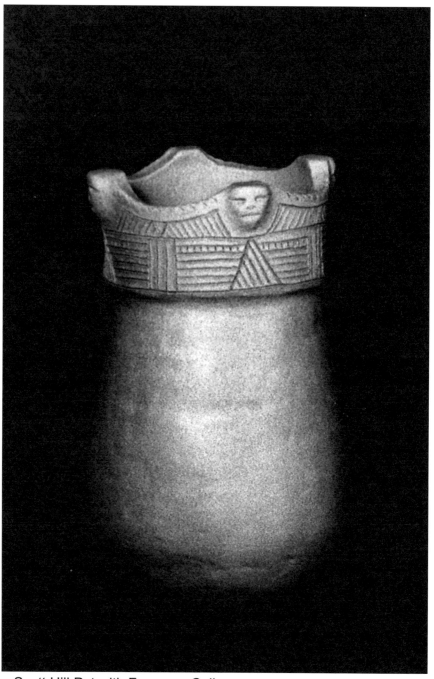

Scott Hill Pot with Faces on Collar

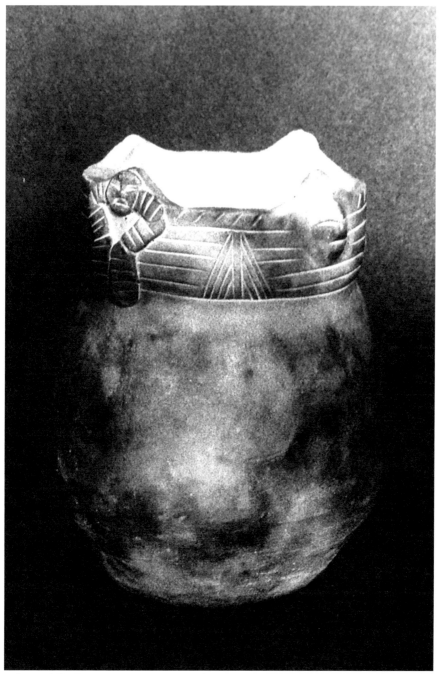

Scott Hill Pot with Figures on Collar

7. Brenda John

Brenda John Pot with Squared Collar

Brenda John Incising Pottery

8. **Michael Jones**

Michael Jones coiling a pot

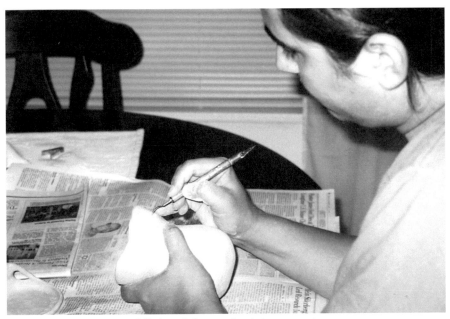

Michael Jones incising a pot

Michael Jones pot with collar with flowers and lines

Michael Jones pot with collar with lines 1

Michael Jones pot with collar with lines 2

Michael Jones pot with faces on collar and incised sky domes

Michael Jones pot with figures and flowers

Michael Jones pot with lines and flowers in background

9. Peter B. Jones

Peter B. Jones Brown Scratched Pot with Lined Collar

Peter B. Jones pot with collar with dots and lines

Peter B. Jones pot with collar with faces and lines 1

Peter B. Jones pot with collar with faces and lines 2

Peter B. Jones pot with collar horizontal lines

Peter B. Jones pot with scalloped collar

Peter B. Jones pot with tall collar

10. **Rose Kerstetter**

Rose Kerstetter pot with collar with human figure 1

Rose Kerstetter pot with collar with human figure 2

Rose Kerstetter pot with collar with human figure 3

Rose Kerstetter pot with collar with lines and faces

Rose Kerstetter pot with human figures and lines

Rose Kerstetter pot with lines and collar
11. **Amanda Malcolm**

Amanda Malcolm pot with collar with lines 1

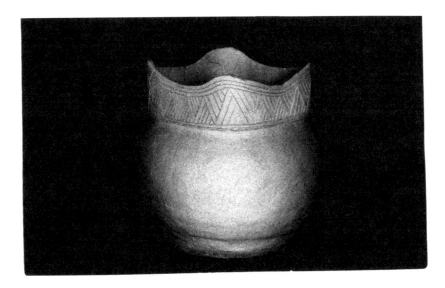

Amanda Malcolm pot with collar with lines 2

Amanda Malcolm working

12. Kenneth B.Metoxen

Kenneth B.Metoxen portrait with pot

Kenneth B. Metoxen pot with collar

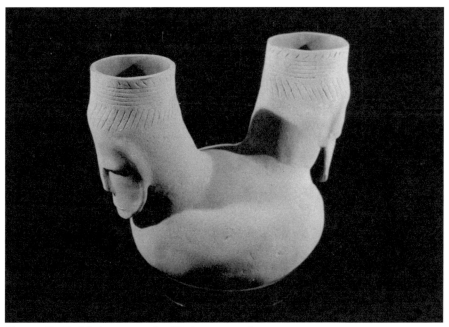

Kenneth B. Metoxen pot with two openings

13. Don Monture

Don Monture Portrait

Don Monture Pot with Collar with Lines 1

Don Monture Pot with Collar with Lines 2

Don Monture Pot with Feet

14. Ron Monture

Ron Monture Portrait

Ron Monture Pot with Figures

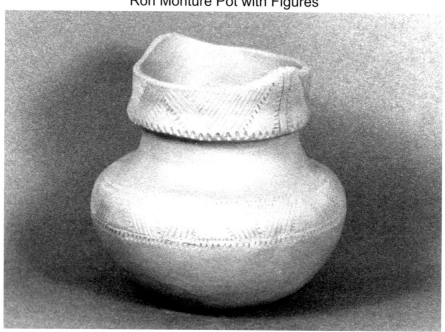

Ron Monture Pot with Collar with Lines

Ron Monture Pot with Pointed Collar

Ron Monture Pot with Square Collar

15. **Carol Moses**

Carol Moses Portrait

Carol Moses pot

16. Roger Perkins

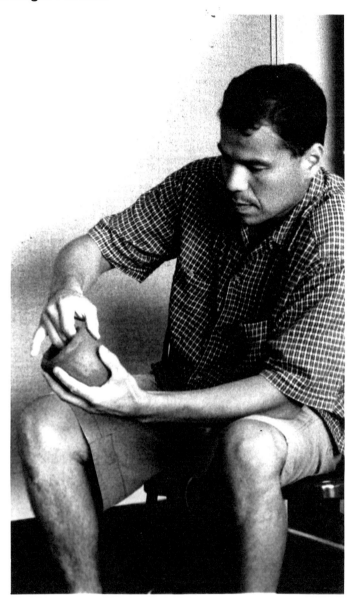

Roger Perkins portrait

Roger Perkins pot 1

Roger Perkins pot 2

Roger Perkins Tall Pot

17. **Molly Melchert Powless**

Molly Melchert Powless Portrait

Molly Melchert Powless Pot with Designs

Molly Melchert Powless Pot with Lines and Dots

Molly Melchert Powless Pot with Turtle

Molly Melchert Powless Pot with Small Collar

18. **Diane Shenandoah (Oneida, NY)**

Diane Shenandoah figure

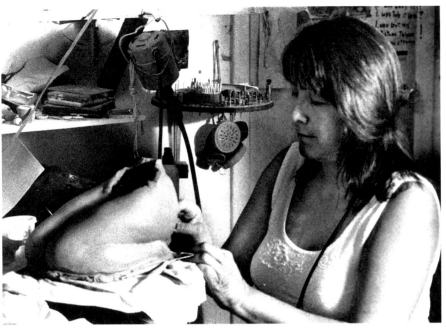

Diane Shenandoah portrait while working

Diane Shenandoah three pots

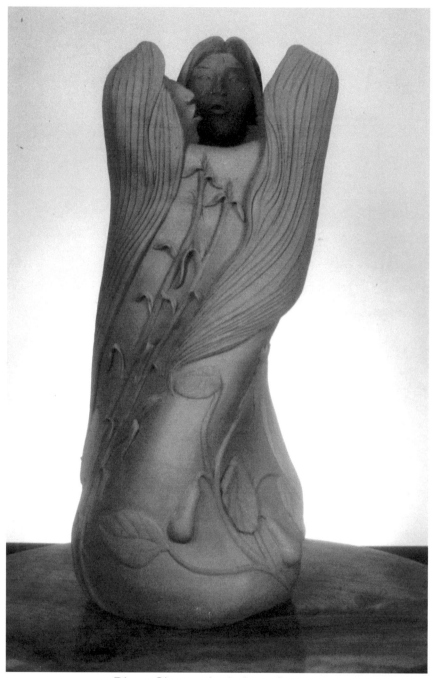

Diane Shenandoah three figures

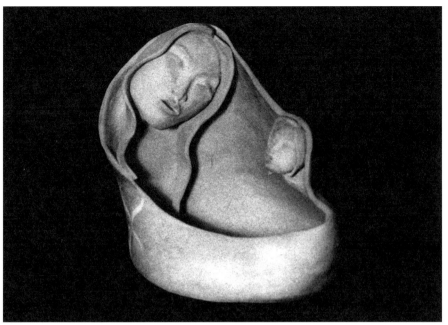

Diane Shenandoah two faces

19. **Dan Skenadore**

Dan Skenandore Portrait while Working

Dan Skenandore Pot with Collar with Designs

Dan Skenandore Pot with Wide Collar

Dan Skenandore Short Pot with Collar

20. **Sara Smith**

Sara Smith Jar with Openwork Flowers

Sara Smith Jar with Turtle, Sun

Sara Smith Jar with White Pine and Roots

Sara Smith Pot with Turtle, Tree, and Wampum

21. **Steven T. Smith**

Steven T. Smith Pot with Carved Eagle, Turtle, and Wolf

Steven T. Smith Pot with Carved Turtle and Pine

Steven T. Smith Pot with Relief Face and Birds

Steven T. Smith Pot with SW Designs

Steven T. Smith Pot with Three Sisters and Bear

Steven T. Smith Pot with Turtle

Steven T. Smith Spider Pot

Steven T. Smith Vase with Carved Figures and Turtle

22. **Leigh Smith**

Pot by Leigh Smith ⟶
Sold to Margaret Thatcher, 1983

Leigh Smith Vase with Loon

Leigh Smith Jar with Lacrosse Player and Eel

Leigh Smith Jar with Seated Women

Leigh Smith Jar with Woman and Wolf

Leigh Smith Pot with Archer on Map

Leigh Smith (Mohawk)
Dancer pot, wheel thrown, 1985

Leigh Smith Pot with Male Dancer and Grouse

Leigh Smith Vase with Bald Eagle and Wolf
23. **Santee Smith**

Santee Smith Black Pot with Elder

Santee Smith Pot with Black Wolves

Santee Smith Canteen with Hummingbird and Flowers

Santee Smith Vase with Sun Face and Corn

Santee Smith Vase with Woman and Wolves

24. **Semiah Smith**

Semiah Smith (child) Holding Small Black Pot

25. **Sylvia Smith**

Sylvia Smith Lidded Vessel with Heron in Wetland Scene

Sylvia Smith Small Wide-Mouth Pot

26. Jennifer Stevens

Jennifer Stevens Pot with Bear Paw on Collar

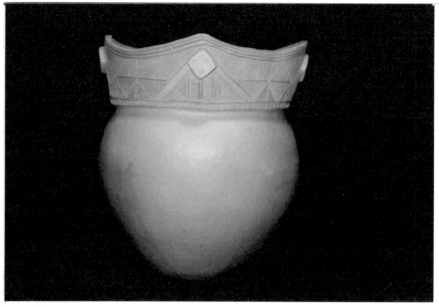

Jennifer Stevens Pot with Fine Lines on Collar

Jennifer Stevens Pot with Neck and Collar

27. Tammy Tarbell-Boeh

Tammy Tarbell-Boeh Beaded Strawberry Pot

Tammy Tarbell-Boeh Pot with Turtles

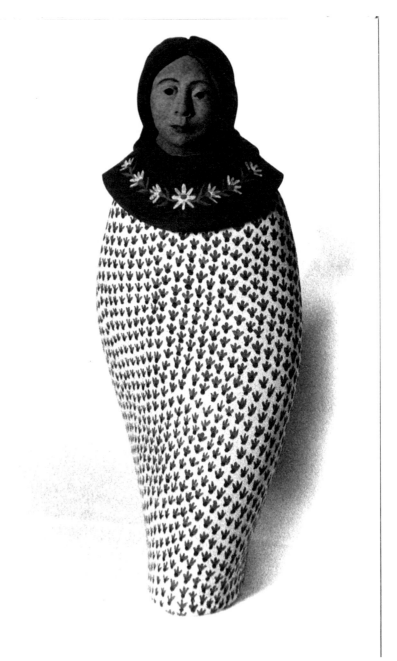

Tammy Tarbell-Boeh Female Figure with Calico Dress

Tammy Tarbell-Boeh Figure of Woman with Beaded Fringe Shawl

Tammy Tarbell-Boeh Figure of Woman with Beaded Fringe Shawl 2

Tammy Tarbell-Boeh Jar in form of Female Figure on Turtle

28. **Elda Smith** (deceased)

Elda Smith Brown Pot with Cut-Out Flowers

Elda Smith Jar with Openwork

29. **Oliver Smith** (deceased)

Oliver Smith (Mohawk)
Vase, wheel thrown, n.d.

Oliver Smith Black Pot with Surface Texture

30. **Darlene Smith** (deceased)

Darlene Smith Four Small Pots with Collars

Darlene Smith Pot with Bird

Darlene Smith Pot with Bird Flying Across Moon

Darlene Smith Pot with Deer in Relief

Darlene Smith Pot with Clan Birds

31. **Murray Antone** (deceased)

Murray Antone Jar with Bear

Murry Antone Pot with Bear

Murry Antone Pot with Geometric Lines

Murry Antone Pot with Linear Designs

Murry Antone Pot with Turtle and Bear

Murry Antone Pot with Wolf

Murry Antone Pot with Wolf & Cub

Murry Antone Pot with Zigzag

BIBLIOGRAPHY:

Abbott, Clifford
Personal Communication, 2007

Antone, April
Interview, 1996

Bell
Interview, 1986

Case, Richard G.
Onondaga Pottery. Syracuse, NY: Everson Museum of Art, 1973.

Engelbrecht, William Ernst
A Stylistic Analysis of New York Iroquois Pottery. Ann Arbor:
University of Michigan Microfilms International, 1986

Engelbrecht, William Ernst
"The Reflection of Patterned Behavior in Iroquois Pottery
Decoration," *Pennsylvania Archaeologist* 42, 3, 1972: 1-15.

Harrington, M.R.
The Last of the Iroquois Potters. Albany: University of the State of
New York, 1909. [From N. Y. State Museum and Science Service
Bulletin 133, Fifth Report of the Director, 1908] pp. 222-227, 10
leaves of plates.

Hauptman, Lawrence and McLester, III, L. Gordon.
The Oneida Indian Journey from New York to Wisconsin, 1784-1860.
Madison, WI: University of Wisconsin Press.1999: 64.

Hertzberg, H. W.
The Great Tree and the Longhouse: The Culture of the Iroquois. New
York: Macmillan, 1966, 6th ed..

Hewitt, John Napoleon Brinton.

Iroquoian Cosmology: First Part. Washington D.C.: Government
Printing Office, 1903: 221-254

Holmes, William Henry
Twentieth Annual Report, Bureau of American Ethnology, 1898-1899.
"Aboriginal pottery of the Eastern United States". Washington, DC:
Government Printing Office, 1903: 233-843.

Johannsen, Christine and Ferguson, John P., editors.
Iroquois Arts: A Directory of a People and Their Work. Warnerville,
NY: Association for the Advancement of Native North American Arts
and Crafts, 1983: viii

Jones, Peter B.
Personal Communication, 2013

Lee, Andrew; guest curator and editor Vanessa M. L Vogel
*Keeping the Living Tradition of the Iroquois Alive: The Pottery of
Peter B. Jones.* Clinton, NY: Emerson Gallery, Hamilton College,
Spring 1994.

Lorenz, Carol Ann and Jones, Peter B.
Photo archives. 2004.

MacNeish, Richard S.
*Iroquois Pottery Types: A Technique for the Study of Iroquois
Prehis*tory. Ottawa, Canada: Department of Resources and
Development, National Parks Branch, 1952.

Metoxen, Kenneth B.
Personal Communication, 2010

Peterson, Polly Ann; guest curator and editor Vanessa M. L Vogel
The Living Art of Diane Schenandoah: Spiritual Messages in Clay.
(Dreams and Visions from the Woodlands: Contemporary Artists of

the Iroquois and Ojibwa, Exhibition Note No 7). Clinton, NY: Emerson Gallery, Hamilton College, 1995.

Ritchie, William A.
Archaeology of New York State. NY, NY: Knopf Doubleday, 1965.

Rushing III, W. Jackson, Editor.
Bernstein, Bruce
Native American Art in the Twentieth Century: Makers, Meanings, Histories. NY, NY: Routlege. 1999: 57-68.

Sagard-Théodat, Gabriel. Editor: George H. Wrong. Translator: H. H. Langton. *The Long Journey to the Country of the Hurons*. Toronto, Ontario: The Champlain Society. 1939: 108-109.

Seneca-Iroquois National Museum
Out of the Ashes: The Death and Rebirth of Iroquois Pottery.
Exhibition brochure, Seneca-Iroquois National Museum, Salamanca, NY, 1999.

Smith, Sara
Personal Communication, 1985

Smith, Sylvia
Personal Communication, 1996

Smith, Wanda
Personal Communication, 2001

White, John K.
Personal Communication, 1985

Wonderley, Anthony
"Oneida Ceramic Effigies: A Question of Meaning," *Northeast Anthropology* No. 63, Spring 2002: 23-48.

Wonderley, Anthony

Oneida Iroquois Folklore, Myth, and History: New York Oral Narrative from the Notes of H.E. Allen and Others. Syracuse, NY: Syracuse University Press, 2004.

ARTIST STATEMENT

The first glimpse of a traditional Iroquois pot in the New York State Museum in the 1960s changed my life forever! I had been searching for an interesting career and finally discovered myself when I enrolled in Ceramics with Ralph Pardington at the Institute of American Indian Arts in Santa Fe, New Mexico, in 1977, and graduated at age 60 with an Associate Degree in Ceramics and 3-Dimensional Design.

Holding a traditional-style Iroquois pot always takes me back to the time when my ancestors made clay cooking pots. I quickly developed a strong interest in learning about the early pottery and its firing methods.

A 1983 grant from the Southwestern Association on Indian Affairs presented an opportunity to begin the learning process, originally planned as a guide for a beginning Iroquois potter "isolated" in the Southwest. After the interviews at Six Nations Reserve were completed, I realized I also had gathered enough material for a story on the revitalization of Iroquois pottery.

The formula apparently was not passed down through oral tradition when the Iroquois women stopped making clay pots and began using the black kettles with handles offered by the incoming Europeans in the fast-growing fur trade of Seventeenth Century America. No reference to material used for waterproofing the pots was found except for Harrington's 1908 report, which is covered in my notes on Culture in Clay–The Revitalization of Iroquois Pottery.

A revitalized tradition often returns in a changed form. Iroquois Pottery is being created in a decorative style for gift-giving and bringing beauty into our daily lives as well as commemorating special events. The original shapes with incised collars keep me in touch with where I come from; and the forms are adapted to complement the visions from the elegant ancient sherds that forever inspire the *Haudenosaunee*–People of the Longhouse.

Oneida potter Rose Skenandore Kerstetter (Tsi'stala: Shining Star), Turtle Clan, lived on the Oneida Nation Reservation, Oneida, Wisconsin, and has been creating traditional and contemporary pottery for over thirty years. Following graduation at age 60 in 1979 with an Associate of Fine Arts degree in ceramics and three-dimensional design from the Institute of American Indian Arts, Santa Fe, New Mexico, Kerstetter received a fellowship from the South Western Association on Indian Arts (Santa Fe) to purchase printed materials on the technology of creating and firing traditional Iroquois pottery, available only in widely-scattered ethnological materials. The 1983 grant included a survey to be made of contemporary Iroquois potters. Other grants followed to complete the research that developed into the story of the recent revitalization of Iroquois Pottery. Kerstetter has completed a book, CULTURE IN CLAY, about the revitalization of Iroquois pottery, and a related DVD on CREATING TRADITIONAL POTTERY OF THE IROQUOIS, including firing.* At the age of 102, Kerstetter remains devoted to strengthening and preserving the tradition in the Oneida community.

POTTERY EXHIBITS include Haudenosaunee Living Treasures, Fenimore Art Museum, Cooperstown, NY; Out of the Ashes, Seneca Iroquois National Museum, Salamanca, NY; Speaking the Words, Sharing the Visions, Hartwick College, Oneonta, NY; Earth Visions: Art of the Woodland Peoples, Art Center, Old Forge, NY; Creativity is Our Tradition, Three Decades of Contemporary Indian Art, Institute of American Indian Arts Museum, Santa Fe, NM; Museum of the Iroquois Indian opening, Howes Cave, NY; Oneida Nation Museum, Oneida WI; Native Peoples of New York: Portraits of Continuity and Change (permanent display), New York State Museum, Albany NY; Wisconsin Indian Arts Fest/Eau Claire WI; WI Indian Arts Fest/LaCrosse WI; Featured Artist '88, Catskill Gallery, Catskill, NY; Red Cliff Cultural Institute, Bayfield WI; American Indian Community House Gallery, New York, NY; 20th Anniversary IAIA Retrospective, Santa Fe, NM; Native American Center for the Living Arts opening, Niagara Falls, NY.

COLLECTIONS: Seneca Iroquois National Museum; the Oneida Nation Museum; Foster Gallery, University of WI/Eau Claire; University Library, University of Wisconsin/Stevens Point; Institute of American Indian Arts; Museum of the Iroquois Indian; New York State Museum; Maxwell Museum of Anthropology and private collections in the United States, Denmark, and Japan.

AWARDS: Community Spirit Award '01 and Cultural Capital Fellowship '04, First Peoples Fund; Traditional Native Arts Apprenticeship Grant, WI Arts Board, Oneida Nation Arts Program and the Oneida Nation '02; Artistic Excellence Fellowship, WI Arts Board, Oneida Nation Arts Program and the Oneida Nation '99; 1st Place awards: WI Indian Traditional Arts Invitational, University of WI/Stevens Point, WI '87; WI Indian Arts Fest/University of WI/LaCrosse, WI, Juror's Award of High Merit '84; Fellowship, Southwestern Association for Indian Arts '83; 1st Place Award, Student Exhibit, Heard Museum '80.

PUBLICATIONS: *Haudenosaunee Living Treasures,* New York Historical Association; *Iroquois Voices, Iroquois Visions, A Celebration of Contemporary Six Nations Art,* Bright Hill Press.

* As a sole grantee of a grant from the Oneida Nation Arts Program to produce the DVD, Kerstetter is the sole producer of the DVD.

ABOUT THE AUTHOR:

Rose Kerstetter had been working on this book for almost thirty years. These are stories of potters, some of which are still with us, some who are not. Some of the stories and photos are from long ago, and Rose had to contend with the time that has passed, but Rose was 100 years old when she met the publisher of Phia Studios and thought it was time to finish the story.

Published by Phia Studios © Teelia Pelletier

ISBN: 978-0-9988513-5-8

Made in the USA
Columbia, SC
14 November 2024

46465468R00106